ED TAPPER

A PATTERN OF LOOKS

STOAT BOOKS

A PATTERN OF LOOKS

ISBN: 978-1-918724-03-5

POCKET SERIES

03

First published 2026

Edited by Leona Franke

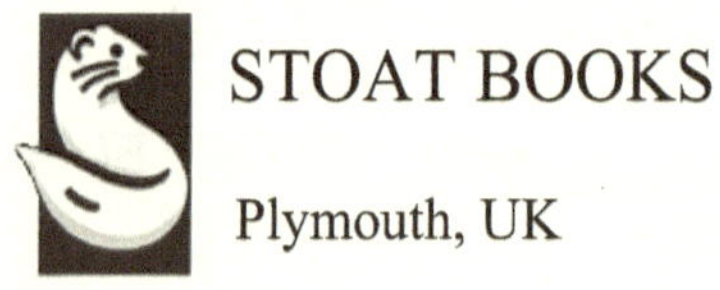

ED TAPPER

A Pattern of Looks is both guide and meditation, a book about seeing as much as sketching. Ed Tapper invites the reader into the life room, where every mark is an act of choice and every drawing a dialogue between artist, model, and the lived history that shapes perception.

This is a work forged from practice, philosophy, and pedagogy — a text that insists drawing is not simply representation, but conversation: between body and paper, failure and experiment, doubt and discovery. Tapper writes with candour and wit, grounding technical advice in the lived stories of looking.

There are no shortcuts here, only attention, integrity, and the restless joy of making art that listens back.

OTHER BOOKS:

Easy Peelers, 2022

Spoke Reflector, 2024

A POCKET GUIDE TO LIFE DRAWING

A Drawing is a Pattern of Looks

‘*Make Craft your sail and let Art be the breeze on the azure seas of do as you please.*’

Ed Tapper

Life Drawing is a conversation between the artist and the model. A drawing emerges from the gap between your provenance and intent between past and future, between all the artwork you have ever made and all the artwork you will make. You may think you are drawing the life model, but you are not; you are drawing your perception of the model.

I once had an epiphany. I had been trying to achieve a likeness using different techniques and conceptual approaches, trying a variety of media and innovating a few of my own. My drawings had recently been subjected to a strange recurring motif: horizontal bars kept appearing behind the figure, sometimes even penetrating the figure but what could this mean? I was thinking about this as I climbed the granite steps to the life room then – of course! How could I have not seen it? I was drawing the horizontal steps to the studio. I was drawing the life model, but my perception of the model had been informed by a simple everyday experience. If that was true, then every artwork I make must appear as a consequence of lived experience. You may choose where to look and how to draw, but the trajectory of your intent can be traced back through the provenance of your life. What is *your* story? What influence does this have on your work?

'I don't mistrust reality, of which I know next to nothing. I mistrust the picture of reality conveyed to us by our senses, which is imperfect and circumscribed. Our eyes have evolved for survival purposes. The fact that we can also see the stars is pure accident.'

Gerhardt Richter

The Model Speaks

The model is not an inanimate object; they are your most important collaborator in the process of looking and drawing. The model has a provenance too, they have practical needs, and they have a particular presence that can be encouraging and challenging or frustrating. Choose your model well and look after them.

Humans have an infinite variety of forms to be explored in the life room, in an infinite combination of artists, media and approach. Every model has their own unique aesthetic of beauty; it is up to you to find it. The life model has generously given you this pause, allowing you to focus on observation. The world outside may be chaotic, but the life room is still and silent and naked.

Why Life Drawing?

The human body is the unit measure of our existence. We are curious about ourselves and about others. When you look at a life drawing there are always three people present: the artist, the model, and the viewer. Come back and look at your drawing again years later and you will be surprised how much it has changed you will remember precisely what you were thinking and feeling when you drew it. You have created coordinates for time travel.

Drawing is easy, all you have to do is put the right marks down in the right place and remove the wrong ones but of course learning how to do that is the Art.

Media

To be concise I am going to focus on drawing with pencil or charcoal on paper but obviously you can draw with anything – smoke, tears, snail slime, fireworks, go ahead, don't let me stop you. Drawing with Indian ink or a stick of carbon is great but once you make a mark you can't get rid of it. Most of the process of drawing is editing. Doubt and hesitation are your constant companions; you can stop and completely change your mind at any point, so whatever you do should be just as easy to undo.

I like to draw with a thick twig of charcoal or a soft pencil – 2B, 3B or 4B and a putty rubber that I can sculpt into a point for precision or roll into a ball to pat the surface. But that's just me, if you want to make a life drawing you need to find your own means.

'If you are a poet, you will see clearly that there is a cloud floating in this piece of paper. Without a cloud there will be no rain; without rain the trees cannot grow, and without trees we cannot make paper. The cloud is essential for the paper to exist. If the cloud is not here, the sheet of paper cannot be here either.'

Thich Nhat Hanh

Paper is Space

A brand-new untouched sheet of paper is not empty; it is filled with infinite possibilities. As soon as the first marks appear, they define the space the drawing will occupy. Is it the space of a domestic interior? Is it the close, intimate space of a lover? Is it the space of an epic landscape? Is it cosmic space? All these questions are answered with the first blemish.

Every drawing is confined by the edges of the paper. Your drawing will always be a dialogue with the shape, proportion, and proximity of the edges. Edges are important, but most people don’t see them. Photographers know this, their subject is the whole Universe, and their problem is deciding where to put the edges of their picture.

What do you do when you are drawing and an edge arrives, unexpectedly cutting off a head or a limb? Well you add more paper; glue another sheet on and keep going. What happens if you tear a hole in the paper and go right through the surface? Some of Frank Auerbach's most moving drawings are a mosaic of paper patches, layers of averted disasters and corrected mistakes.

'I am always doing that which I cannot do in order that I learn how to do it'

Pablo Picasso

Getting Ready

Set up early. If you are working at an easel, make sure you have plenty of space behind you so you can stand back and see what you are doing.

Get comfortable. Your gaze will constantly be moving from drawing to model and back again. Position your body so that you move your head as little as possible; life drawing can literally become a pain in the neck.

Get rid of distractions. Noisy phones, clutter, conversation, temperature, toilet breaks, faulty equipment, lighting, privacy, the list is endless, but you can shorten it.

Get organized. Broken pencils are not a problem if you are holding two more in your other hand. Once you start drawing, you need to hang on to your train of thought.

'Art takes shape in spite of it all, rarely and always unexpectedly; art is never feasible.'

Gerhardt Richter

Starting

Draw before the model arrives. The life room is unoccupied before and after the model, so why not explore it? When the model appears, they will step into a conversation that has already begun.

Draw the model before they begin to pose. Have you chosen the right media? Are you in the right position? There is still time to change your mind.

First impressions. Dorothy Parker called this 'the first fine careless rapture'. Try to respond to the model instinctively, glance without thinking and draw accordingly.

Start with no preconceptions. Everything should be possible before some possibilities become probable, and some probabilities become inevitable. The process of making Art is a series of choices, maximize your choices.

Cultivate your instincts then learn to trust them. Look at the decisions other artists have made by carefully drawing their work and learn from their courage. Follow your nose and go where you find it most interesting, not where everyone else goes. Fashion, perfection and good taste are your enemies.

When the first few marks appear, you will need to think about scale. Is the drawing too big or too small? What adjustments do you need to make? Do you need to begin again? Do you need a bigger sheet of paper?

'Ever tried. Ever failed. No matter. Try again. Fail again. Fail better.

Samuel Beckett

Drawing

Failure is a healthy part of the process; failure is not defeat. Examine your failures carefully for clues and create strategies to avoid repeating them.

Keep your mistakes but get rid of your cliches.

Don't try to make a beautiful drawing, make an honest one.

Draw with absolute candour; you have no one to impress but yourself.

Every decision you make is a fork in the road. Do you keep this mark or get rid of it? Is this an important part of the drawing or is it just scaffolding to be removed later?

The drawing continues to accumulate decisions until it reaches critical mass. You may find you have created two or three possible outcomes struggling against each other to be seen on the same piece of paper. At this point you must choose the one with the most integrity not the most beautiful be ruthless and destroy the others. Sacrifice the dull for the interesting even if it means you must deny the complete for the partial however they are not lost you may revisit them in your next drawing.

Look at the life model but listen to your drawing. What is your drawing about? It could be about the balance of shapes or the collision of shapes, forms in harmony or antagonistic forms, beautiful ugly or ugly beautiful, structure or surface, weight or weightlessness, flesh can be transformed into liquid or smoke. Your drawing will suggest a theme if you listen to it. Once the drawing is convinced of its own character, how can you best help it to emerge? Often the answer is to step aside and let it find its own way.

Draw a new elbow every day. Observe your own habits and preferences and find new pathways. Most people will always start by drawing the head first but this is a trap, why not begin by drawing the negative space, or the ankles or the navel? why not start by drawing from a space inside the ribcage? Overfamiliarity with a technique or approach that guarantees success can only bring boredom and the worst thing you can do in Art is bore yourself.

Draw through a drawing. Every drawing is part of a complex, evolving series of other drawings, it is informed by your previous work, and it will inspire your future work, it carries your intent while you are working on it, and then you move on. Learn from it, but don't linger too long. Drawings should cohere then co-there.

Take a break. If you are in a life room with other people, have a look at what they have been drawing. How have they solved the same problem you have been struggling with? What mistakes have they made that you can avoid? Come back to your drawing with fresh eyes and you will see things you had not noticed before. Howard Hodgkin would paint a canvas then turn it to face the wall sometimes for days sometimes for years then he would turn it around and see it again almost as if it were the first time.

There is beauty in economy; don't decorate for the sake of it. Superfluous marks are unnecessary but be careful, I am not suggesting bare austerity should be your goal. Sometimes a casual mark in the background, one that seems to serve no practical purpose can actually define the space; and without it the drawing falls apart. Use a scrap of torn paper to cover up a mark and see how your drawing looks before committing to remove it.

What is a good drawing? A good drawing is not necessarily a satisfying one. It may be perplexing or baffling, it might not make sense for many years, and if you are lucky, it may even take you to the very edge of your practice and allow you to peer over. Other people may share a consensus about your "best" work but for you a good drawing is an important drawing.

There is no such thing as mark making, there is only look making. A tree may create a beautiful mark on a wall with its branches but the tree has no artistic intent and no artistic provenance to share. An artist may put the tree in a gallery, they might even put a whole orchard, but the tree now serves the artist's intent and their provenance. We are surrounded by intriguing artistic inspirations; choose wisely.

An artist is the integrity of their choices. Artificial Intelligence can offer an infinite number of alternatives it will produce what is most popular using algorithms that access vast databases, but all it can ever offer is pastiche. In life drawing an artist is not just saying 'this is what a body looks like' they are also saying ‘this is how it feels to have a body’. An artist is more than the sum of their influences, they are original, and embracing originality is key. Artists create the first manifestations of the future.

‘Art is not what you see it is what you make others see’

Edgar Degas

Finishing

If you are lucky a drawing may be resolved. This means its component parts have reached a point in the process where nothing more needs to be added and removing anything would damage its coherence. This does not mean every element is in perfect balance however, it could mean they are in tension or collision or opposition or any number of compelling relationships.

Sometimes as they reach the final stages of an artwork, I have seen students gripped by a strange fear – 'what if I ruin it?' They have completed 90% but recoil from committing the last 10% to paper in case they spoil their precious life drawing and overwork it. I say do 110% and ruin it utterly only that way will you learn how to add just enough.

When a drawing is finished it needs to be looked at. It is good to see your drawing in relation to its predecessors and later, its descendants. It may wish to join a group of similar images, or it may want to remain unique. Either way it must be carefully studied preferably on the wall of a studio where it can join other such provocations. Cherish the Art which baffles you it is the most useful.

Sometimes drawings need to brew like beer, hidden away in the dark. Enjoy them too soon and they are flat and tasteless but given time, they will reward you with a rich complexity you were initially oblivious to. Sometimes you may be alarmed or even horrified by what you have drawn it may feel as if another hand has reached in and taken over. Good. Now you are getting somewhere.

The Group Crit.

Learning how to fail is a key part of every artist's development. Surround yourself with the trusted support of like-minded people who are also struggling to draw. Their invaluable objectivity is the antidote to your subjective failure. When you fail they will help you see the positives in your work where you can see only mistakes. Then a week later it will be someone else's turn to fail and your duty to help them.

'A painting is finished when it looks back at you'

Pablo Picasso

Digital Media

When photography was first introduced some portrait painters despaired fearing that this would be the end of painting. Others saw the photograph could become a useful tool in the process of painting or even free the artist from realism altogether and allow them to explore new worlds. During the 1970s orchestras were advised to throw away their musical instruments and replace them with a single synthesiser now of course every orchestra has a synthesiser in its ranks.

Photograph your drawings and you will free them from the confines of paper space. In digital space they become plastic, mutable and multiple. Take pictures of your drawing as it develops and you create a forensic record of your decision-making process. Catalogue your work and you will find hidden intentions, subtle currents of narrative you were perhaps unaware of in the physical confines of a portfolio.

Using editing software is akin to print making; all choices exist in layers that can be corrected, undone or discarded. Your original life drawing is now just the starting point for an entirely new art form, which in turn fundamentally changes the way an artist must approach life drawing in this century. Knowing a life drawing can be projected, animated, worn, or 3D printed expands the range of artistic possibilities and informs the artist's intent at the very point they enter the life room and for the first time the charcoal touches the paper.

How to Dissect a Painting

Here are a set of critical tools you can use to find out how a painting works. They have limited application for sculpture and video but you can use them to examine photographs, drawings and prints.

Composition

What compositional devices has the artist used?

Look for alignments, geometric shapes or simple patterns hidden in the work. These often come in three different forms:

- Vertical and horizontal devices when used together produce a sense of calm or stillness as seen in the work of Georges Seurat.
- Diagonal compositions have a dynamic sense of movement and energy such as in the work of Carlo Carrà.

- Combining all three compositional devices can create a sudden moment of drama in a still space, as in the work of Piero della Francesca.

Whatever compositional devices you discover in a painting, the most important question to ask is why? Why has the artist chosen to do this? What do you think they are trying to do?

Tone

What tones has the artist used?

Stare at the painting through half closed eyes so that minor details disappear and you are left looking at different tonal values.

- Where is the painting darkest?
- Where is it lightest?
- Where are the middle tones?
- Where are the areas of greatest tonal contrast?

The tones vary across the painting in a very specific manner. Why has the artist done this? What are they trying to emphasise? What does this suggest?

Colour

Look at the range of colour. What colour system has the artist used?

- Is it a restricted palette of muted colours?
- Is it monochrome?
- What colour relationships can you see?

- Do you see primary colours, secondary colours, or complementary colours?
- Why do you think the artist made these colour choices?

Complementary colours, especially when used in combination with tonal contrast, can often emphasise an important area of the painting. What do you think the artist is doing with colour? Why?

Imagery

What imagery has the artist chosen?

- Perhaps the artist has eliminated all imagery such as in the work of Kazimir Malevich

- Perhaps it is crammed with imagery such as in the work of Richard Dadd or Paula Rego.
- Perhaps the artist has chosen imagery that remains ambiguous such as in the work of Juan Miro.

Why has the artist chosen these images? Does this kind of imagery occur elsewhere in this artist's work? What do these images relate to?

Biographical Context

What was happening in the artist's life at the time they made this painting?

- What does that tell you about the choices they made?
- What are they preoccupied by at this moment in time and why?

- Where does this art work fit in the story of this artist's life?

For example, Vincent Van Gogh painted his '*Sunflowers*' (1888) for his friend Paul Gauguin.

Historical Context

What was happening in the world at the time the artist painted this artwork?

- How did this impact on the artist's life?
- How did this affect the development of their work?
- Did the work of other artists influence their work?
- What historical impact did this artwork have?

For example, '*The Piano Lesson*' (1916) by Henri Matisse is a portrait of his son, painted before he left to fight in World War I.

Meaning

If you have reached this stage; having looked at a painting and thoroughly examined the artist's use of composition, tone, colour, imagery, and researched the biographical context and the historical context, then you should now have enough information to make an informed guess at the meaning of the artwork. What exactly is the artist trying to do here? How successful do you think they have been?

Finally, if you apply this set of criteria to your own work what will you discover?

'You know, Phaedrus, that is the strange thing about writing, which makes it truly correspond to painting. The painter's products stand before us as though they were alive, but if you question them, they maintain a most majestic silence. It is the same with written words; they seem to talk to you as if they were intelligent, but if you ask them anything about what they say, from a desire to be instructed, they go on telling you just the same thing forever.'

Socrates, on ekphrasis to Phaedrus

www.ingramcontent.com/pod-product-compliance
Lightning Source LLC
LaVergne TN
LVHW051023080826
845145LV00009B/2771

* 9 7 8 1 9 1 8 7 2 4 0 3 5 *